WHY WE
Walk

Siena's Stories

Book 2

Illustrated by Shannon Wilvers

Why We Walk

Siena's Stories 2

ISBN: 978-1-989579-37-4

MotherButterfly Books

MotherButterfly
Books

www.motherbutterfly.com

To all my school classmates, teachers and staff.
Thank you for making the destination as fun as the journey.

My name is Siena.

My parents named me after a very pretty city in Italy.

I live in Ottawa, the capital of Canada.

8:30 a.m. Monday morning ...

Time to leave for school.

On school days, my daddy and I get dressed for our walk to school.

Rain or shine,
snow or sleet.

My daddy pulls my red wagon to carry my backpack.
Or me, if I get tired.

In the winter, I wear my...

snowsuit

toque

mitts

and
boots.

Daddy wears his broad brim winter hat...

snow boots,

gloves,

and **3** jackets!

Even our wagon has a winter kit.

In the spring and fall,
our jackets and shoes are lighter,
but Daddy and I
always
wear a hat on our heads.

He tells me we must protect our skin from the sun.

I think he also likes wearing a hat because he is losing his hair.

Everyday we talk, laugh and play a game.
The first to see a squirrel yells:

Squirrel!!!!

and wins the game.

I know Daddy sees them most of the time but lets me win.

We pass through a large park attached to the school.

One day we saw a cardinal.

One day we saw a bluejay.

One day a cat followed us for a while.

As I got older, I noticed that few children walked to school.

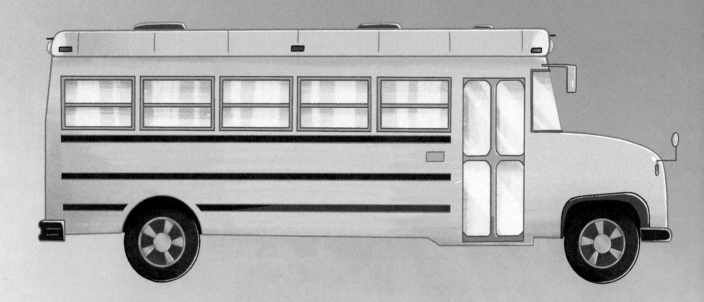

Many kids on our street took the bus or were driven to school by their parents.

One day, I asked my daddy:

Why do we walk?

As we neared the school door, we passed a long line of cars, trucks and buses waiting to drop children off at my school

He pointed to the long line of vehicles.

"See the exhaust coming from the tail pipes?"

"Yes,"
I said.

"That exhaust is hurting the planet we live on," stated Daddy.

"So, every time someone walks to school, the less we hurt the planet. A planet that you and your friends will inherit from your parents."

I look up at Daddy and smile.

"Mommy told me you also really like spending time with me."

Daddy looked down and smiled as well.

A squirrel darts out of a nearby bush.

We both yell:

Squirrel!!!!

at the same time and laugh.

I hold my daddy's hand as we finish our walk to school.

About the Author

Siena is a real Canadian kid who likes long walks and making up stories with her father. Both of whom choose to create these books somewhat anonymously.

About the Illustrator

Shannon Wilvers is a Canadian illustrator who loves drawing things on her computer. While she mostly draws and colours digitally, she also likes to experiment and play with different mediums such as watercolour.In her spare time, she enjoys learning new things and watching cartoons. Her current favourites are "Avatar: The Last Airbender" and "Kipo and the Age of Wonderbeasts". She is based in New Brunswick where she lives with her dog, Lucy.

Get FREE books!

Go to :
motherbutterfly.com

If you enjoyed this book, please leave a review online at Goodreads & Amazon.

This is the best way for authors to share their stories with readers.
We appreciate your help!

Thank you!

Manufactured by Amazon.ca
Bolton, ON

26517117R00021